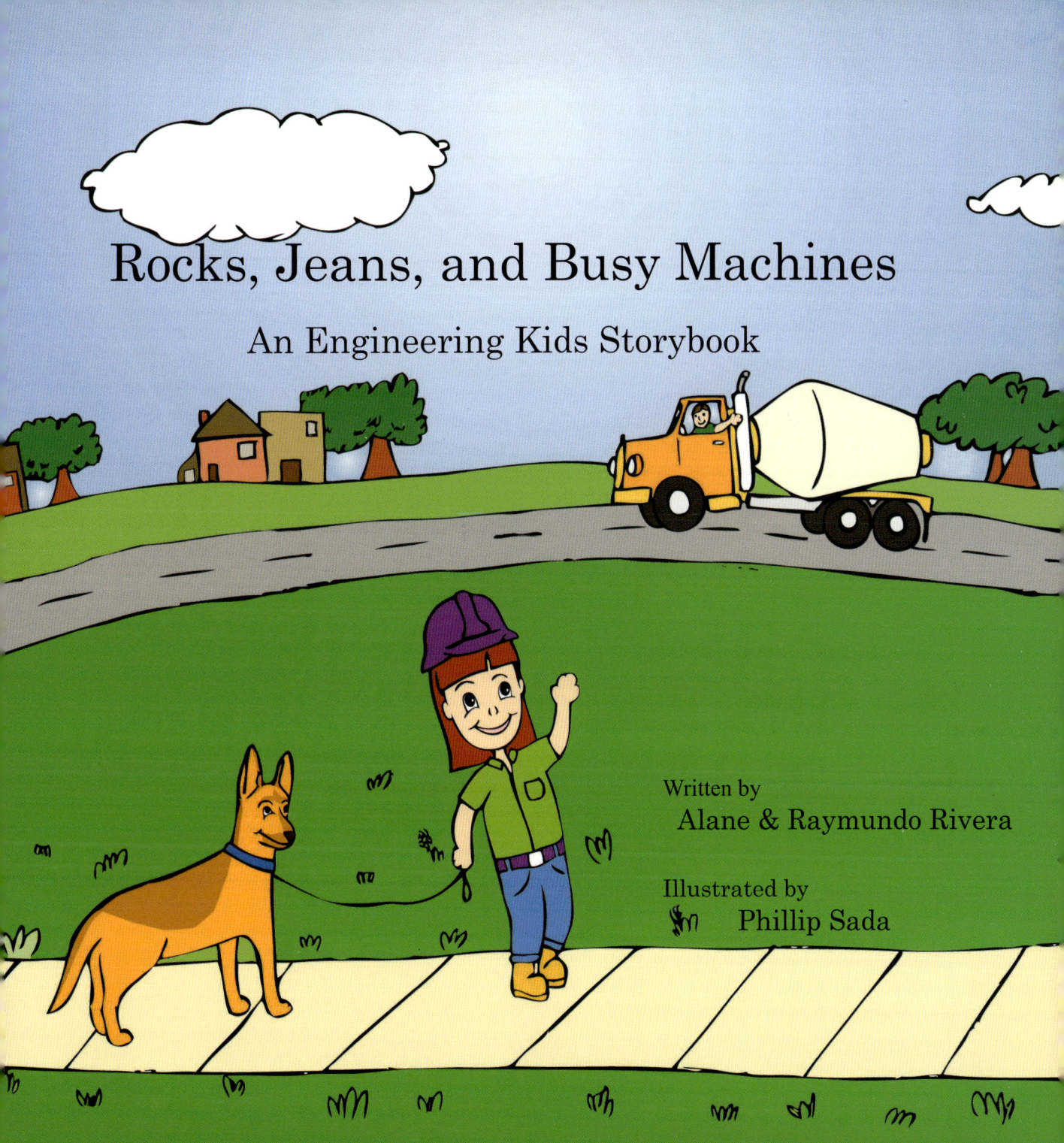

First Edition Copyright © 2009 by Alane and Raymundo Rivera

All rights reserved. No part of this publication may be reproduced, stored in a retrieval system or transmitted in any form or by any means, electronic, mechanical, photocopying, recording or otherwise, without the prior written permission of the publisher.

Library of Congress Catalog Number:
ISBN 13: 978-0-9801695-0-8
Published by Rivera Engineering, San Antonio

Printed in Korea

Structural engineers help people by designing bridges, towers, and buildings such as schools, houses, and stores.

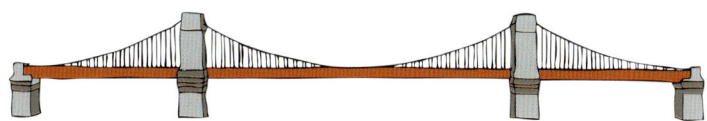

Violet

Pedro

Mike

Meet the Engineering Kids!

Darla

Doc

This Engineering Kids Storybook Belongs

To:

_____

The warm sun beamed brightly through the bedroom window when Violet awoke.

"What a perfect day to go to the park!" she thought as she stretched in her bed. "I think I will invite my friend Pedro to come, too."

Violet climbed out of her bed and stood before her closet. "Hmmm, what should I wear today?" Violet asked her dog, Doc. "Jeans it is!" she exclaimed, pulling a pair of neatly-hung blue jeans from the hanger.

After she dressed, Violet and Doc raced outside and walked down the street to Pedro's house.

"Can Pedro come to the park to play?" Violet asked Pedro's mother.

"Of course!" she said. "Be careful crossing the street," she called out as Violet and Pedro marched around the corner.

As Pedro and Violet neared the park, they came upon a construction site, which buzzed with activity. Large machines grumbled as they dug into the ground with huge claws. Other machines beeped loudly as they carried building materials from one place to another.

"These workers are constructing a new building," Violet announced matter-of-factly. "It's going to be very tall!"

As they watched, one truck rumbled to the front of the construction site.

"Look at the big barrel on the back of that truck!" cried Pedro.

"That's a concrete truck," explained Violet. "The barrel in the back mixes the concrete and keeps it from getting hard until it's ready to be used."

"What is concrete?" asked Pedro.

"It is a mix of sand, small rocks, water and cement," Violet said, pointing. "The cement acts like glue to keep everything together. It is like the sand that was at the beach your family visited last summer!"

"Each ingredient is not very strong by itself, but after they are mixed together, they become concrete, which is very hard and very, very strong," Violet explained.

"That is why it is used to make the building. The building will need to hold people, desks, chairs, and everything else that will be inside," said Violet.

"The engineer who designed the building will make it strong enough to stand up to the most powerful wind you can imagine, and even heavy snow!" She continued. "It is the engineer's job to make sure the building is safe for the people inside during all kinds of weather, and even earthquakes and floods."

Violet and Pedro continued on their way to the park, and soon arrived at a sturdy brick bridge.

"This bridge must have been created by an engineer!" exclaimed Pedro.

"Yes!" said Violet. She explained. "The engineer had to imagine all the different types of cars and trucks that would travel across it, and make the bridge strong enough to carry them all!"

The park was just around the corner from the bridge. As Violet and Pedro arrived, they were joined by their friend Mike and his big brother. They all raced to the monkey bars and began to swing across.

"Whoever holds on the longest is the winner!" shouted Violet, dangling from the rail.

"I hope the engineer made these bars strong enough to hold all of us!" shrieked Pedro.

"Me too!" shouted Mike's brother. They all laughed as they kicked their legs and swung back and forth.